FINCHES

BACKYARD BIRDS

Lynn Stone

The Rourke Corporation, Inc.
Vero Beach, Florida 32964

PHOTO CREDITS
© Marie Read: cover, pages 4, 18, 21; © Tom Ulrich: pages 7, 10, 13; © Tom Vezo: pages 8, 12; © Lynn M. Stone: page 15, title page; page 17 courtesy Aspects, Inc., Warren, RI

COVER ART:
James Spence

EDITORIAL SERVICES:
Penworthy Learning Systems

Library of Congress Cataloging-in-Publication Data

Stone, Lynn M.
    Finches / by Lynn M. Stone.
       p. cm. — (Backyard birds)
    Includes index
    Summary: Describes the physical characteristics, habitats, and behavior of different kinds of finches, including the purple finch, house finch, and grosbeak.
    ISBN 0-86593-469-X
    1. Finches—Juvenile literature. [1. Finches.] I. Title II. Series. Stone, Lynn M. Backyard birds.
QL696.P246S785 1998
598.8'8—dc21   98–4727
                                                     CIP
                                                     AC

Printed in the USA

TABLE OF CONTENTS

FINCHES

Finches are small perching birds that like to eat seeds. They use their beaks to crack seeds open.

Many finches are among our best-known backyard birds. The American goldfinch is the state bird of Iowa, New Jersey, and Washington. The purple finch is the state bird of New Hampshire.

The house finch always lived in the West. In the 1950's house finches were set free in New York City. Now they live all over the East, too.

The purple finch, the state bird of New Hampshire, lives in many eastern states.

WHAT FINCHES LOOK LIKE

Finches are small, active birds. They are from 3 3/4 inches to 6 inches (10 to 15 centimeters) long. The size depends on the **species** (SPEE sheez), or kind, of finch.

Sparrows are cousins of finches. Like sparrows, most female finches are brown. Male finches, though, have patches of reddish or yellow feathers.

The male American goldfinch, with his jacket of black, yellow, and white, is the most colorful of North American finches. In winter, even the male goldfinch wears only dull yellow **plumage** (PLOO mij), or feathers.

The male goldfinch wears a bright yellow jacket in spring, summer, and early fall.

WHERE FINCHES LIVE

Finches are a widespread family of birds. Wherever you live in North America, one or more finch species live nearby.

Both the purple and house finches like woodlands. But they're often seen in suburbs and around farms.

The American goldfinch lives in fields and in the weeds by country roads. The goldfinches of the Southwest—the lesser and Lawrence's goldfinches—like dry, open places.

The rosy finch of the Northwest is a mountain-loving bird.

Weeds attract seed-eating finches like this female pine siskin.

THE FINCH FAMILY

Many kinds of birds in the finch family live in North America. Seven species called "finch" are found north of Mexico. Some birds in the finch family are not called "finch." The pine siskin, for one, is more like goldfinches than is the house finch.

The birds known as redpolls and crossbills and some grosbeaks are also finches. The largest finch in North America is the evening grosbeak, measuring 7 1/4 inches (18 1/2 centimeters) from bill to tip of tail.

The evening grosbeak, just 7 inches long, is the biggest of American finch-like birds.

Female finches, like this goldfinch, do not have the same bright colors as the males.

Cassin's finches live in the evergreen forests of the West. They migrate south in autumn, like many finches.

FINCHES IN THE BACKYARD

As a group, finches are tame. They visit backyards all year, and they love **feeding stations** (FEE ding STAY shunz), or birdfeeders.

Unlike some birds, finches will use many kinds of feeders. They will peck at food on the ground, too.

Finches like backyards even without feeders. Finches can find seeds in almost any plant. The goldfinch likes garden flower seeds and thistles. Thistle feeders attract goldfinches, too.

14

Backyard berries, like these crabapples, are tasty winter foods for this house finch and other birds.

BACKYARD FOOD FOR FINCHES

Setting a table for hungry finches is easy. They eat parts of many plants. Purple finches like pumpkin seeds, safflower seeds, millet, nutmeats, and even bread.

The American goldfinch likes hemp, millet, nutmeats, and sunflower seeds, along with thistle seeds. Pine siskins love millet, sunflower seeds, hemp, and nutmeats.

House finches take sunflower seeds, as do evening grosbeaks. Evening grosbeaks also like peanuts and safflower seeds.

Goldfinches crowd a backyard thistle feeder.

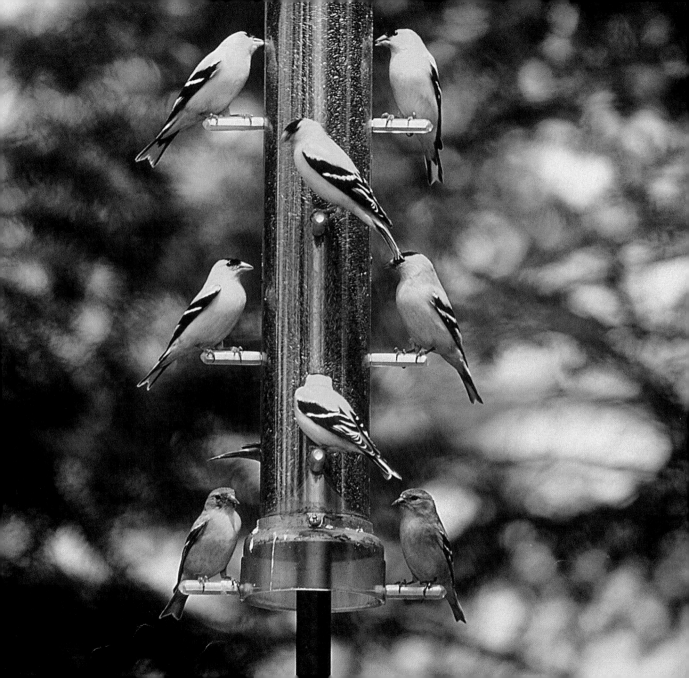

FINCH HABITS

The number and kinds of finches in your yard will change with the seasons. That is because most finches move south as winter nears. None of the finch species nest in Florida. Each fall, though, some purple finches, pine siskins, and American goldfinches **migrate** (MY grayt), or travel, south to spend winter in ice-free Florida,

Goldfinches are singers as well as travelers. Their *per-cic-o-ree* song sounds like "Just look at me!"

Called "thistle bird," this male goldfinch plucks thistle seeds.

FINCH NESTS

Finches and their cousins may have different nesting habits. House finches and sparrows will nest almost anywhere. They even nest on large buildings.

Goldfinches are more choosey. They like leafy trees or bushes near thistles. Goldfinches wrap their nests with the silk of spider webs.

The purple finch and pine siskin build their nests in conifers. **Conifers** (KAHN uh ferz), like pine and spruce, are trees whose leaves look like green needles.

A mother goldfinch sits on her eggs in a nest that looks like a cup.

BABY FINCHES

A mother finch usually lays four or five eggs. She keeps the eggs warm by sitting on them in the nest.

The eggs hatch after about two weeks of **incubation** (IN kyuh BAY shun), or mother's warmth. The parent finches feed their babies.

Goldfinch babies grow by eating mushy seeds. The babies' parents crush the seeds in their beaks and swallow them. Then the parent finch brings up the soft seeds into its mouth. The mushy seeds are fed to the babies.

Young finches fly when they are about two weeks old.

Glossary

conifer (KAHN uh fer) — any one of several kinds of trees with needle-like leaves, such as pines and spruces

feeding station (FEE ding STAY shun) — a place where people put food for birds; a birdfeeder

incubation (IN kyuh BAY shun) — keeping eggs warm before they hatch

migrate (MY grayt) — to travel to a distant place at the same time each year

plumage (PLOO mij) — the feathers on a bird

species (SPEE sheez) — within a group of closely related animals, one certain kind, such as a *purple* finch

INDEX

FURTHER READING:

Find out more about Backyard Birds with these helpful books and information sites:

• Burnie, David. *Bird*. Knopf, 1988
• Cooper, Jason. *Birds, the Rourke Guide to State Symbols*. Rourke, 1997
• Mahnken, Jan. *The Backyard Bird-Lover's Guide.* Storey Communications, 1996
• Parsons, Alexandra. *Amazing Birds*. Knopf, 1990
• *Field Guide to the Birds of North America*. National Geographic, 1983
• Cornell Laboratory of Ornithology online at http://birdsource.cornell.edu
• National Audubon Society online at www.audubon.org